CHRISTIANITY
YOUR FREE
PASSPORT
TO
HEAVEN

Harold W. Decksheimer

*Wishing you God's
special blessings
Harold Decksheimer*

A Schiel & Denver Paperback

Christianity Your Free Passport To Heaven

First published in 2011 by Schiel & Denver Publishing Limited
10685-B Hazelhurst Drive Suite 8575
Houston, Texas USA 77043

www.schieldenver.com

ISBN 978-1-84903-067-0

Copyright © Harold W. Decksheimer 2011

Printed in the United States of America and United Kingdom.

Typeset by Schiel & Denver Publishing Limited.

All papers used by Schiel & Denver Publishing are natural
recyclable products made from wood grown in well-managed
forests. The manufacturing processes conform to the
environmental regulations of the country of origin.

DEDICATION

This book is dedicated to my wife Jean who has spent many hours by herself while I worked on this project. Also to our children and spouses, grandchildren and spouses and great grandchildren. My hope is that they will also pass it on to future generations. I look forward to seeing them all in Heaven.

ACKNOWLEDGEMENTS

A special "thank you" to Pastor Keith Reisdorf, Senior Pastor of First Lutheran Church, Kelowna, B.C., for editing and endorsing this book.

Material as found in *Lutheran Worship*: Apostles Creed, the Lord's Prayer and Evening & Morning Prayers from Luther's *Small Catechism*.

From Luther's *Small Catechism* © 1986, 1991 Concordia Publishing House. Used with Permission. www.cph.org.

Scripture taken from the HOLY BIBLE, NEW INTERNATIONAL VERSION, Copyright © 1973, 1978, 1984 International Bible Society. Used by Permission of Zondervan Bible Publishers

CONTENTS

FOREWORD

"… Always be prepared to give an answer to anyone who asks you to give the reason for the hope that you have. But do this with gentleness and respect."
1 Peter 3:15

I love when people speak words of hope. As an optimist, I believe hope is the fundamental quality that delivers, in our present moment, exactly what we need to live and breathe through whatever is before us. But if we rely on ourselves for this "hope", we are short changing the possibility and power that lies beyond ourselves, and missing the source that delivers what we cannot. The pages you are about to read are an expression of hope that

Harold Decksheimer believes is vital for truly living. Out of love for family, friends, acquaintances and those unknown to him, but known to God, Harold has created this book. Having been Harold's pastor for the past 12 years, it is my pleasure to endorse his work. Harold has been a leader of the church I serve for over forty years. It is from his servant's heart that he has written this work as a means of serving Jesus and others within the human family who may or may not be familiar with the principals upon which his faith is founded. This book is an expression of Harold's faith and love for others. This love has enabled him to spend the time necessary to share his hope not only for the living of this life but an eternal future founded in the grace and mercy of God through Jesus. Harold focuses on the most important aspects of the faith without getting caught up in details which might occupy a theologian's energy. "Christianity –Your Free Passport To Heaven", presents a hopeful truth for your life and mine that can be trusted and believed.

I know Harold's prayer for this work is that it would find itself in the hands of anyone who God desires this work to connect with, that you may know the security which Harold has enjoyed over a life time.

My prayer is that God would use this book to bless you through Harold's efforts as he shares an interpretation of Jesus' passion and love for all humanity.

It is with joy that I recommend the following pages – may they ground you in a hope and life beyond anything this world offers.

With joy,
Keith Reisdorf, pastor

PREFACE

There has been a lot of information published over the years about Christianity and other different religions. My purpose for writing this booklet is to explain CHRISTIANITY in simple terms so that it can be easily understood and embraced by those who are willing to accept the direction and promises of GOD as given to us in the Holy Bible. This is also my personal way of sharing God's good news of Salvation to as many people as possible. God wants all people to hear this good news so we can share ETERNAL Life with Him in HEAVEN.

I have been a Christian all of my life and now, at the age of seventy seven, I feel compelled to share this good news especially with all of my family, relatives, friends and as many others as possible through this booklet.

Toward the end of this book, you will have the opportunity to claim your personal PASSPORT TO HEAVEN. This book is directed to both Christians and non-Christians. For the non-Christian it will show you God's love and the promise of free Eternal Life in Heaven which has already been paid for by His Son Jesus. For the Christian, it will take away any doubts that you may have regarding your faith. You will be re-assured of God's Grace, that all of your sins are forgiven through faith in God and believing that Jesus is your Lord and Savior. I have read a survey that indicated that as many as fifty percent of Christians are not absolutely sure that they indeed have Eternal Life. This book will give you all the scriptures and promises of God so that you can have full one hundred percent assurance of Eternal Life in Heaven.

This is a very serious and important subject which you should not put off. Death can come at any time and then it will be too late. It is my hope and prayer that you will take the time to read this book and allow the Holy Spirit of God to work Faith in your heart.

I hope to see you in Heaven.

Your friend in Christ,
Harold Decksheimer
March 21, 2010

CHAPTER ONE:

CHRISTIANITY– INTRODUCTION

Christianity is based on the Holy Bible which reflects God's love for us through His Son Jesus. In early Bible history, God gave us the Ten Commandments so that we would have strict guidelines to live by. However, He also knew that all mankind was sinful and not capable of being perfect. According to James 2:10 when we break any one part of God's law, we violate God's will and thereby are guilty of His whole law. Therefore we are guilty of sin which separates us from God. Romans 3: 23&24 confirm that we are all sinners. However, God in love and mercy toward all sinners, provided a plan of salvation for us by putting all our SINS upon Jesus. Christianity is all about Jesus. It is the Gospel (good news) of God concerning His Son and what God has done in Christ Jesus for all humans. We cannot earn our way into Heaven, nor can we buy our way into Heaven. It is a FREE GIFT from GOD to all who will receive it. One of the key verses in the Holy Bible is John 3:16. These are the very words of JESUS.

> "For God so loved the world that He gave His one and only Son, that whoever believes in him shall not perish but have eternal life."

3

We could also add verse 17. "For God did not send his Son into the world to condemn the world, but to save the world through him." Verse 16 is often referred to as the Gospel in a nutshell because it summarizes God's plan of salvation for everyone. Yes, Christianity is all about Jesus. He is the promised Savior for all mankind. He fulfilled the prophesies of the Old Testament, lived a perfect life, then was crucified on a cross on our behalf to fulfill God's plan of Salvation for all people. Then as promised by God, Jesus miraculously returned to life on the third day to prove that He was indeed the Son of God. He was more powerful than death. He did all of this on our behalf, so that we could be guaranteed ETERNAL LIFE through HIM. The scriptures are very specific, and teach that we are saved by God's Grace, not by good works.

Ephesians 2:8-9 makes this very clear as follows: "For it is by grace you are saved, through faith and this not from yourself, it is the gift of God. Not by works, so that no one can boast." Also, Romans 3:20-24 tells us that God loves us so much that if we, in faith, believe and trust in Jesus as our Lord and Savior, we will have eternal life as a free gift. We can not earn it by doing good deeds.

Martin Luther, who was a Catholic monk some 500 years ago, tried to figure out how to please God. He would pray for hours, he would fast, but nothing seemed to work or give him peace. He never gave up and continued to search the scriptures and found the truth just as we have seen in the scriptures above. The Holy Spirit opened up his mind to fully understand God's plan of salvation which is not determined by what we do, but by what has already been done for him, and for all of us, through Faith in Jesus Christ. This enlightenment changed his life and he reformed the teaching and understanding of the Bible in that we are saved by Faith in Jesus, not by good works, as was being taught and understood at the time.

It seems to me that it is time to re-start this Reformation in 2010 and let everyone know this good news. ETERNAL LIFE IN HEAVEN is a FREE GIFT from GOD, Who wants all people to be saved. Unfortunately, the vast majority of people think that going to Heaven after death is based on doing good deeds and trying to keep the Ten Commandments. If salvation is based on good works and keeping the Ten Commandments we would fail every day because by nature we are all sinners and fall short of God's laws. If it were up to us to "try hard" to be good, we would never know if we have done enough, thus having no assurance of Eternal Life. Our thoughts are often messed up, relationships are broken, harmful addictions hurt us, we fail to serve others with love and respect, our thoughts are not always God pleasing, and the list goes on. Romans 3 verses 23 and 24 are very clear that we are all sinners and require God's free gift of Grace. "For all have sinned and fall short of the glory of God, and are justified freely by His grace through the redemption that came by Christ Jesus."

We can not go to Heaven by good works because we are all sinners, which started by one man, Adam, in the Garden of Eden. On our own accord we are not perfect, but Scriptures teach that Jesus is, and through faith in Him and what he did at the cross, God declares us as perfect. We are made sinless or perfect in Jesus, who cleanses us with His perfection on our behalf. <u>This is a gift that God offers to all people by His grace.</u> This is the good news of the Gospel as recorded in John 3:16, Ephesians 2:8, Romans 3:23-24 and many more places in the Bible. Heaven is therefore a free gift from God by grace through faith, but it was actually purchased at a huge cost by Jesus. As God in human flesh, He lived a perfect life for us. He suffered a cruel death on a cross for us. He conquered death by rising to life on the third day and then, after forty days, ascended to Heaven, all recorded in the Scriptures (1 Corinthians 15: 3 and 4). What an awesome sacrifice all done for our salvation to provide life after death. We can all be assured of Eternal Life in Heaven if we believe that Jesus Christ is our Lord and Savior. We need to accept the fact that we are all sinners and repentantly believe that Jesus suffered and died for all of our sins. Some additional scriptures to give us assurance are as follows:

John 14:6 – Jesus speaking to his disciples, said, "I am the way and the truth and the life. No one comes to the Father except through me."

John 11:25 and 26 – Jesus speaking to Martha, said "I am the resurrection and the life. He who believes in me will live, even though he dies; and whoever lives and believes in me will never die."

This is the basis of Christianity. Salvation is not determined by what we do (good works), but what has already been done for us by JESUS, who is the only Savior as promised by God in the Holy Bible. Unfortunately, there are a lot of people in this world who believe that their salvation has to be earned and there are many religions that teach this philosophy. Or they believe it's deserved for trying to be a good person. These are opposite teachings from Christianity, which teaches we are saved by what has already been done. We do not have to go through life wondering if we have done enough. Through faith in Jesus we can say with confidence, "my salvation has been accomplished for me by JESUS CHRIST." Not only do we have the assurance of Eternal Life, we can also embrace this faith in our daily lives. Through faith and trust in God we grow in our ability to be loving, forgiving and accepting toward others. We can reflect our faith by our good deeds toward others. Any good deeds done toward others reflect our thanks to God for His free gift of salvation to us.

Christians are not perfect, our flaws are far too visible, but God cleanses us from all of our faults and shortcomings. We admit our failures to God and He forgives us. When we are weak, we call on God for strength. As a Christian, I'm not holier than thou. I'm just a simple sinner who has received God's free grace of forgiveness. Our purpose and goal is to serve God and others to the best of our ability, but when we fail, God is always there to forgive us as we repent. It is our faith in God that saves us, not our perfection, which we are unable to attain. We become perfect in His sight when we repent of our sins and He forgives us according to the promises of His word. Our goal is to refrain from sin or evil and turn to serving God by serving others in need. Paul the apostle makes this clear in Romans 6, especially in versus 14 and 15, which reads, "For sin shall not be your master because you are not under law, but under grace." What then? Shall we sin because we are not under law but under grace? By no means.

CHAPTER TWO:
WHO IS JESUS?

The Scriptures teach, Jesus is the son of God and true Savior for all mankind. He is true God in that He is part of the Triune God (Father, Son and Holy Spirit). However, He also became true man, being conceived by the Holy Spirit and born of the Virgin Mary so that God's plan of salvation could be accomplished.

HIS BIRTH

His coming into the world was first announced by God after Adam and Eve fell into sin in Genesis 3:15. This was about 2,500 years before Jesus was born. The Prophet Isaiah also announced the future birth of Jesus about 800 years before Christ's birth in Isaiah 9:6. "For unto us a child is born, to us a son is given, and the government will be on his shoulders. And he will be called Wonderful, Counselor, Mighty God, Everlasting Father, Prince of Peace." Just before His birth, an angel sent by God spoke to Mary regarding the birth of Jesus in Luke 1:35. "The Holy Spirit will come upon you, and the power of the Most High will overshadow you. So the holy one to be born will be called the Son of God." Also, in verse 31, "You will be with child and give birth to a son, and you are to give him the name Jesus."

An angel also appeared to Joseph in Matthew 1:20-21 and said, "Do not be afraid to take Mary home as your wife because what is conceived in her is from the Holy Spirit. She will give birth to a son, and you are to give him the name Jesus, because he will save his people from their sins."

When Jesus was born in a stable in Bethlehem, God sent an angel to some shepherds to announce this special event. Luke 2, verses 8 to 14 reflects this good news as follows: "And there were shepherds living out in the fields nearby, keeping watch over their flocks at night. An angel of the Lord appeared to them, and the glory of the Lord shone around them and they were terrified. But the angel said to them, "Do not be afraid. I bring you good news of great joy that will be for all the people. Today in the town of Bethlehem a Savior has been born to you; he is Christ the Lord." Christians continue to celebrate the birth of Christ each year during the Christmas season. We celebrate the birth of the promised Savior of the world.

HIS MINISTRY

Jesus began His ministry at the age of thirty, however, before He started teaching and performing miracles, He went to be baptized by John the Baptist as recorded in Matthew 3:13-17. At Jesus' baptism, John publicly announced the arrival of the Messiah and the beginning of His ministry of teaching and serving humanity. Jesus did not need to be baptized but in verse 15 He said, "It is proper for us to do this to fulfill all righteousness."

Jesus then began His ministry of preaching, teaching and performing miracles to prove that He was indeed God's Son, the promised Savior. He chose twelve disciples to assist Him. He trained them so that they could continue His ministry after His return to Heaven.

HIS MIRACLES

During His three year ministry, Jesus continued to prove that He was the Son of God by performing hundreds of miracles. In Matthew 4:23-24, we get a glimpse of some of the miracles performed as He started His ministry. We read as follows: "Jesus went throughout Galilee, teaching in their synagogues, preaching the good news of the kingdom, and healing every disease among the people. News about Him spread all over Syria and people brought to Him all who were ill with various diseases, those suffering severe pain, the demon-possessed, those having seizures, and the paralyzed, and He healed them."

Here is just a sample of some other miracles.
- Turned water into wine at the wedding feast in Cana, John 2:1-11
- Rebuked the storm, Luke 8:22-25
- He restored Lazarus back to life, John 11:38-44
- Healing of the ten men with leprosy, Luke 17:11-19
- Feeding of the 5000, Matthew 14:15-21

- He walked on water, caught more fish than the nets of His disciples could hold and the list goes on.

Of course the greatest miracle was His Resurrection on the third day following His crucifixion. Matthew 28:1-10, Mark 16:1-18, Luke 24:1-2 and John 20:1-10. These miracles attest to Jesus being the Son of God. (not just human, but divine)

HIS PROMISES

The Bible lists many promises from Jesus which bring us peace, comfort and assurance as we struggle through our earthly life, knowing that He is our personal Savior. I have selected a small cross section of promises to help in understanding the love and compassion Jesus has for all people.

- Matthew 11:28-30 – "Come to me, all you who are weary and burdened, and I will give you rest. Take my yoke upon you and learn from me, for I am gentle and humble in heart, and you will find rest for your souls. For my yoke is easy and my burden is light."

- John 11:25-26 – "I am the resurrection and the life. He who believes in me will live, even though he dies; and who ever lives and believes in me will never die.

- John 14:2 – "In my Father's house are many rooms. I am going there to prepare a place for you."

- John 14:6 – "I am the way and the truth and the life. No one comes to the Father except through me."

- Romans 6:23 – "For the wages of sin is death, but the gift of God is eternal life in Christ Jesus our Lord."

- 1 John 1:9 – "If we confess our sins, he is faithful and just and will forgive us our sins and purify us from all unrighteousness."

- Mark 16:16 – "Whoever believes and is baptized will be saved, but whoever does not believe will be condemned."

- Revelations 2:10B – "Be faithful even to the point of death, and I will give you the crown of life." (Eternal Life)

- 2 Peter 3:9 – "The Lord is not slow in keeping his promise, as some understand slowness. He is patient with you, not wanting anyone to perish, but everyone to come to repentance."

God's promises give us hope and comfort for this life. We can trust in His promises because God fulfilled all His promises about the coming of the Savior. We can also trust that He will fulfill His present promises.

HIS DEATH AND RESURRECTION

The death of Jesus was a necessary sacrifice to fulfill God's plan of salvation for all mankind. According to 2 Corinthians 5:21, He was sinless, but " God made Him to be sin for us so that in Him we might become the righteousness of God." Jesus sacrificed His life for all of our sins. He was our substitute and has fully atoned for all of our sins. Here are just a few passages from the Bible to confirm this.

- 1 John 1:78 – "and the blood of Jesus, his son, purifies us from all sin."

- 1 Peter 1:18-19 – "For you know that it was not with perishable things such as silver or gold that you were redeemed from the empty way of life handed down to you from your forefathers, but with the precious blood of Christ, a lamb without blemish or defect."

- 2 Corinthians 5:15 – "And he died for all that those who live should no longer live for themselves but for him who died for them and was raised again."

As Christians we annually celebrate the death and resurrection of Jesus during the Easter season. On Good Friday we remember the suffering and pain which Jesus endured on our behalf. He showed His unfailing LOVE to us by suffering and dying on the cross for payment of all of our sins. This was no ordinary death. It was marked with special events which reinforce that He was in fact the Son of God and true Savior of the world. We read the following from Matthew 27:50-51 and 54. "And when Jesus had cried out again in a loud voice, he gave up his spirit. At that moment the curtain of the temple was torn in two from top to bottom. The earth shook and rocks split. When the centurion and those with him who were guarding Jesus saw the earth quake and all that had happened, they were terrified, and exclaimed, 'Surely he was the Son of God.'"

We move forward to Easter Sunday and rejoice in the good news. The tomb is empty. Jesus again proves that He is the Son of God. He has conquered death, which no other person on earth has done.

Again, an angel appears to announce to the women who came to the tomb that Jesus has risen from the dead. This is recorded in Matthew 28:1-6, Mark 16:1-7, Luke 24:1-8 and again in John 20:10-18.

This is the good news of Christianity. Jesus, the Son of God, has risen from death on the third day as was promised by God the Father. Here are two more scriptures confirming the Resurrection of Jesus.

- 1 Corinthians 15:3-5 – Paul is writing to the church in Corinth. "For what I received I passed on to you as of first importance, that Christ died for our sins according to the Scriptures, that he was buried, that he was raised on the third day according to the Scriptures and that he appeared to Peter, and then to the twelve."

- John 21:27-29 – Jesus speaks to Thomas. "Put your finger here; see my hands. Reach out your hand and put it into my side. Stop doubting and believe." Thomas said to him, "My Lord and my God." Then Jesus told him, "Because you have seen me, you have believed, blessed are those who have not seen and yet have believed."

HIS ASCENSION

Jesus spent forty days with His disciples after His resurrection. During this time He prepared His disciples to carry on His Ministry. In Luke 24:44-49 Jesus talks to His disciples. "This is what I told you while I was still with you: everything must be fulfilled that is written about me in the Law of Moses, the Prophets and the Psalms." Then he opened their minds so they could understand the Scriptures. He told them, "This is what is written: The Christ will suffer and rise from the Dead on the third day, and repentance and forgiveness of sins will be preached in his name to all nations, beginning at Jerusalem. You are my witnesses of these things. I am going to send you what my Father has promised; but stay in the city until you have been clothed with power from on high."

Just before His ascension, Jesus promises to send them the Holy Spirit so that they could witness in different languages. This was fulfilled at Pentecost as noted in Acts 2:1-4. After this promise, Jesus physically ascended into Heaven as recorded in Acts 1:9-11. Again, angels appear to the disciples. In verse 11 we read the following message from the angels, "Men of Galilee," they said, "why do you stand here looking into the sky? This same Jesus, who has been taken from you into heaven, will come back in the same way you have seen him go into heaven."

This completes Jesus' physical life on earth.

HIS SECOND COMING

The date of Jesus second coming is not known. In Mark 13:32, Jesus tells His disciples, "No one knows about that day or hour, not even the angels in heaven, nor the Son, but only the Father," In Matthew 24, Jesus tells His disciples about various signs and events which will happen prior to His return to earth as follows:

> Verse 4-5 – Beware of false prophets who will deceive many.

> Verse 6 – You will hear of wars and rumors of wars.

> Verse 7 – Nation will rise against nation, and kingdom against kingdom. There will be famine and earthquakes in various places.

> Verse 9 – You will be hated by all nations because of me.

Verse 12-13 – Because of the increase of wickedness, the love of most will grow cold, but he who stands firm to the end will be saved.

Verse 14 – And this gospel of the kingdom will be preached in the whole world as a testimony to all nations, and then the end will come.

Verse 29 – Immediately after the distress of those days "the sun will be darkened, and the moon will not give its light; the stars will fall from the sky, and the heavenly bodies will be shaken."

Verse 30-31 – At that time the sign of the son of Man will appear in the sky, and all the nations of the earth will morn. They will see the Son of Man coming on the clouds of the sky, with power and great glory. And he will send his angels with a loud trumpet call, and they will gather his elect from the four winds, from one end of the heavens to the other.

We also read in Paul's letter to the Christians in Thessalonica, Chapter 4:16-18, as follows: "For the Lord himself will come down from heaven, with a loud command, with the voice of the archangel and with the trumpet call of God, and the dead in Christ will rise first. After that, we who are still alive and are left will be caught up together with them in the clouds to meet the Lord in the air. And so we will be with the Lord forever. Therefore encourage each other with these words."

Also, we read this in 2 Peter 3:10-13. "But the day of the Lord will come like a thief. The heavens will disappear with a roar; the elements will be destroyed by fire and the earth and everything in it will be laid bare. But in keeping with his promise we are looking forward to a new heaven and a new earth, the home of righteousness."

Many of the signs mentioned have already happened and some are happening now, nearly 2000 years since Christ ascended into Heaven. God is very patient because He wants all people to be saved. According to 2 Peter 3:8-9, we read the following words of encouragement. "But do not forget this one thing, dear friends: with the Lord a day is like a thousand years, and a thousand years are like a day. The Lord is not slow in keeping his promise, as some understand slowness. He is patient with you, not wanting anyone to perish, but everyone to come to repentance."

Our own death or the end of the world could happen at anytime and so we can be prepared. This could be your last opportunity to receive JESUS as your personal Savior.

SUMMARY OF JESUS

I hope this provides a glimpse of Jesus, the Son of God, who came into this world as the promised Savior of all mankind. We have full assurance from the Scriptures that Jesus is the promised Savior of the world. The apostle Paul confirms this in Philippians 2:8-11. "And being found in appearance as a man, he humbled himself and became obedient to death, even death on a cross! Therefore God exalted him to the highest place and gave him the name that is above every name, that at the name of Jesus every knee should bow, in heaven and on earth and under the earth, and every tongue confess that Jesus Christ is Lord, to the glory of God the Father."

Jesus Himself proclaimed this truth of who He was when speaking to Pilate at His own trial before He was crucified in John 18:36-37. Jesus said, "My kingdom is not of this world. If it were, my servants would fight to prevent my arrest by the Jews. But now my kingdom is from another place."

"You are a king, then!" said Pilate. Jesus answered, "You are right in saying I am a king. In fact, for this reason I was born, and for this I came into the world, to testify the truth. Everyone on the side of truth listens to me."

Jesus fulfilled His purpose for us. This is the good news for all mankind which we are blessed to embrace and share with others. This gives us a real purpose in our lives, which I will expand upon in a later chapter.

CHAPTER THREE:
HEAVEN

What is heaven like? That's a question often asked and for the answer we need to search the Scriptures.

Rev. 7:16 – there will be no more hunger, no thirst and no tears. Can you imagine the joy of Heaven not having to worry about food or water? Rev. 21:6 says we will drink from the spring of the water of life and Rev. 22:2 mentions the tree of life bearing crops of fruit monthly.

There will be no more death, or mourning or crying or pain, for the old order of things has passed away according to Rev. 21:4. In this world we all will die a physical death because we are not divine or perfect which limits us physically, but in Heaven we will all be without sin and therefore will live for all eternity. We will be able to enjoy not only our family and friends but all of the people from all walks of life from all nations who believed in Jesus as their Lord and Savior. All of our aches and pains and all diseases will be gone forever. No doctors or hospitals needed.

Rev. 14:13 tells us that we will rest from our labors. This will be an eternal retirement with heavenly benefits. If you can imagine the most extravagant, all inclusive vacation in this world, it would not even come close to the bliss and radiance provided by God in His Heavenly mansions.

Hebrews 12:22 and Rev. 5:11-12 tell us that we will be in the presence of many thousands of angels who are God's appointed servants.

John 14:2 – Jesus says, "In my Father's house are many rooms; if it were not so, I would have told you. I am going there to prepare a place for you."

That's great news for all Christians, having the promise of Jesus that a place will be ready and waiting for us after our earthly death.

Chapter 21 of Revelations describes Heaven and its size. Here are some of the highlights:

- There will no longer be any seas.
- There will not be a need for the sun or the moon for the glory of God gives it light.

The great street is made of pure gold, like transparent glass. The foundations were decorated with every kind of precious stone and the twelve gates were made of huge pearls. This tells us that Heaven is a beautiful, large place designed and created by God for the eternal enjoyment of all who in faith believe and trust in Jesus as their personal Savior. This is the inheritance that our heavenly Father has promised. We can live in hope and joy knowing that God is waiting for us to join Him when our earthly life is ended. In Heaven we will all be as God first intended us to be before sin came into this world.

CHAPTER FOUR:
HELL OR HADES

Scripture teaches that Hell is a real place. This is the final place of punishment for all unbelievers who have rejected Jesus as their personal Savior and are therefore separated from the promises of God. Rev. 21:8 makes this very clear. "But the cowardly, the unbelieving, the vile, the murderers, the sexually immoral, those who practice magic arts, the idolaters and all liars, their place will be in the fiery lake of burning sulfur. This is the second death." Jesus describes the torment and eternal aspect of hell in a parable, or example, of the rich man and Lazarus in Luke 16:19-31 as follows:

> "There was a rich man who was dressed in purple and fine linen and lived in luxury every day. At his gate was laid a beggar named Lazarus, covered with sores and longing to eat what fell from the rich man's table. Even the dogs came and licked his sores. The time came when the beggar died and the angels carried him to Abraham's side. The rich man also died and was buried. In hell, where he was in torment, he looked up and saw Abraham far away, with Lazarus by his side. So he called to him, 'Father Abraham, have pity on me and send Lazarus to dip the tip of his finger in water and cool my tongue, because I am in agony in this fire'. But Abraham replied, 'Son, remember that in your lifetime you received your good things, while

Lazarus received bad things, but now he is comforted here and you are in agony. And besides all this, between us and you a great chasm has been fixed, so that those who want to go from here to you cannot, nor can anyone cross over from there to us.' He answered, 'Then I beg you, father, send Lazarus to my father's house, for I have five brothers. Let him warn them, so that they will not also come to this place of torment.' Abraham replied, 'They have Moses and the Prophets; let them listen to them.' 'No, Father Abraham,' he said, 'but if someone from the dead goes to them, they will repent.' He said to him, 'If they do not listen to Moses and the Prophets, they will not be convinced even if someone rises from the dead."

The only way to escape this eternal separation is to repent of all of your sins and believe in Jesus Christ as your Lord and Savior. He suffered the punishment of your sins on the CROSS and then conquered death by His resurrection from the dead. He rescued us from eternal death so that we could enjoy the eternal blessings of Heaven with Him. Jesus has been patient and He is still inviting you today because tomorrow could be too late to receive Him. Claim the forgiveness you receive in Christ as yours and to make your choice for ETERNAL LIFE in HEAVEN. There is great joy in Heaven when one person repents of their sins. Jesus tells His disciples in Luke 15: 10 "I tell you there is rejoicing in the presence of the angels of God over one sinner who repents."

CHAPTER FIVE:
DEATH

Through improved medicine and medical treatments we can live longer but death will come for all people on this earth. Death is a definite given. That day could be real soon or, if you're young, it may be a long time. What is important is that we prepare for that day when our physical earthly end comes.

Scripture teaches our belief determines what happens to us when we die. When we die our soul, which is a living spirit, departs from our body. The soul that claims salvation through Jesus goes to Heaven to be with Him. However, the unbelieving soul goes to eternal separation and receives the wrath of God, according to John 3:36. "Whoever believes in the Son has eternal life, but whoever rejects the Son will not see life, for God's wrath remains on him." Also, Hebrews 9:27 says, "Just as man is destined to die once and after that to face judgment." Therefore, Christians need not fear death, since it is a stepping stone to Heaven. It is the beginning of our eternal inheritance to enjoy the beauty and benefits of Heaven, our reward from God for trusting Him and believing in Jesus Christ who died on the cross to take away all our sins and then rose from the dead to defeat eternal death for us.

My hope and prayer is that you are ready for death and know for sure based on Scripture that your soul will go to Heaven. This is my real reason for writing this book, because I want as many people as possible to know the plan God has for all us sinners to be forgiven and to inherit eternal life with Him in Heaven. No one should have to suffer eternal death in Hell. As you read through the rest of this book, you will receive all the necessary information to assure you of Eternal Life in Heaven.

CHAPTER SIX:
THE SACRAMENT OF BAPTISM

Baptism was instituted by Jesus in Matthew 28:18-20 when He was speaking to His disciples. Then Jesus came to them (disciples) and said, "All authority in heaven and on earth has been given to me. Therefore go and make disciples of all nations, baptizing them in the name of the Father and of the Son and of the Holy Spirit, and teaching them to obey everything I have commanded you. And surely I am with you always, to the very end of the age."

Scripture tells us that sin makes us spiritually unclean. To cleanse us from our sinful human nature, God sent His Son to attain forgiveness for us when He willingly suffered a physical death for us on the cross. Then after His miraculous resurrection from the dead, He instituted Baptism as a special means of Grace by using water with the power of God's word.

Water is the external element in Baptism. The word "Baptize" means to apply water by various means such as pouring, immersing, washing or sprinkling.

Jesus says that we must be born again of water and the Spirit when He was teaching Nicodemus in John 3:3-8. The power of God's blessing is to baptize in the name of the Triune God, Father, Son and the

Holy Spirit. By being baptized in the name of the Father and the Son and the Holy Spirit we enter into an intimate and blessed relationship with the Triune God. We literally enter into a covenant relationship with God and are the guaranteed beneficiaries of all the blessings of His Grace.

In Baptism, God promises to be our Heavenly Father and adopts us as His children. This promise is recorded in Galatians 3:26-27. "You are all sons of God through faith in Christ Jesus, for all of you who were baptized into Christ have clothed yourselves with Christ.

There are three major benefits received through Baptism.

1. We receive the forgiveness of sins according to the following Scriptures:
- Acts 2:38 – Peter replied, "Repent and be baptized every one of you, in the name of Jesus Christ for the forgiveness of your sins. And you will receive the gift of the Holy Spirit."
2. We are delivered from eternal death.
- Romans 6:3-4 – The apostle Paul is speaking, "Or don't you know that all of us who were baptized into Christ Jesus were baptized into his death? We were therefore buried with him through baptism into death in order that just as Christ was raised from the dead through the glory of the Father, we too may live a new life."
3. We receive eternal salvation.

- 1 Peter 3:21 – "and this water symbolizes baptism that now saves you also, not the removal of dirt from the body but the pledge of a good conscience toward God. It saves you by the resurrection of Jesus Christ."
- Mark 16:16 – Jesus is speaking just before His ascension into Heaven. "Whoever believes and is baptized will be saved, but whoever does not believe will be condemned."

INFANT BAPTISM

According to the scriptures, "All nations" are to be baptized which includes men, women and children. There is no mention in the Holy Bible which excludes children from Baptism. Little children are born human, which implies being sinful and we thank God that He has in His wisdom provided salvation for them through infant baptism. We read this from Luke 18:5-17. "People were also bringing babies to Jesus to have him touch them. When the disciples saw this they rebuked them. But Jesus called the children to him and said. "Let the little children come to me, and do not hinder them, for the kingdom of God belongs to such as these. I tell you the truth, anyone who will not receive the kingdom of God like a little child will never enter it."

Christ Himself tells us that children do believe, as recorded in Matthew 18:5-6. Jesus is speaking to his disciples, "And whoever welcomes a little child like this in my name welcomes me. But if anyone causes one of these little ones who believes in me to sin, it would be better for him to have a large millstone being around his neck and to be drowned in the depths of the sea."

It is the Spirit of God who miraculously works faith in both adults and children through Baptism, which is confirmed in Titus 3:5. "He saved us, not because of righteous things we had done, but because of his mercy. He saved us through the washing of rebirth and renewal by the Holy Spirit."

As infants grow older, and are able to understand God's promises regarding His grace, they can affirm or confirm their Baptism as they believe that Jesus died for all their sins. Most Christian churches instruct young children at an early age in Special Classes and   many who claim infant Baptism, have special instruction classes, at ages 12 to 14 approximately, to teach them all the basic Christian teachings. This allows them to understand their Baptism and to make a public testimony of their faith, which they first received at their Baptism.

Adults who were not Baptized as children are usually instructed in God's word and then are Baptized.

SUMMARY

The power and blessings of Baptism come from the promise of God's word, which is in and with the water. We accept it in faith as we do with all of God's promises to us. Through Baptism we enter into a covenant relation with God and are made beneficiaries of all the blessings of His grace. In

Baptism God promises to be our Father and adopts us as His children.

Scripture tells us that we are spiritually unclean. To cleanse us from all our sins, God sent His Son to guarantee forgiveness for us on the cross and he also instituted Baptism as a means to give us His forgiveness.

CHAPTER SEVEN:
THE SACRAMENT OF THE ALTAR

There are several other names for this Sacrament such as Holy Communion, the Lord's Table, Lord's Supper, the Breaking of Bread or the Eucharist.

Jesus instituted this sacrament during the last supper with His disciples on the Thursday night before His crucifixion on the next day (Good Friday). This is recorded in Matthew 26:26-28, Mark 14:22-24, Luke 22:19-20 and 1 Corinthians 11:23-35.

The following is recorded in Matthew 26:26-28. While they were eating, Jesus took bread, gave thanks and broke it, and gave it to his disciples, saying, "Take and eat; this is my body." Then he took the cup, gave thanks and offered it to them saying, "Drink from it, all of you. This is my blood of the covenant, which is poured out for many for the forgiveness of sins."

The visible elements Jesus used were bread and wine. Most Christian churches use the same elements of bread and wine today. The invisible or heavenly elements are the true body and blood of our Lord Jesus Christ which are miraculously received in, with and under the bread and the wine for the blessing or benefit of Christians. As the promised presence of Jesus comes to us, this sacrament is another means of Grace through which we receive the assurance that our sins are forgiven and our faith is strengthened as we are reinforced in our trust in Jesus as our personal Savior. By strengthening our faith, the Lord's Supper also increases our love and trust toward God which helps to lead a God pleasing life.

1 Corinthians 11:28 tells us that it is necessary to examine ourselves before we go to the Lord's Supper so that we are worthy, thereby receiving the blessings offered. Worthy means recognizing our need for forgiveness and the forgiveness offered.

We examine ourselves by admitting that we are sinful and that we have sinned against God and man. We repent of all our sins and ask God to forgive us of all our sins as He has promised through His word and Sacraments. We also ask that he would strengthen our Faith in Him and that He would lead us to serve Him with renewed spiritual strength.

CHAPTER EIGHT:
THE TEN COMMANDMENTS

The Ten Commandments are the Law of God and are recorded in Exodus 20:1-17. This is a brief summary of the Ten Commandments.

1. You shall have no other gods before me.
2. You shall not misuse the name of the Lord your God.
3. Remember the Sabbath day by keeping it holy.
4. Honor your father and your mother, so that you may live long.
5. You shall not murder.
6. You shall not commit adultery.
7. You shall not steal.
8. You shall not give false testimony against your neighbor.
9. You shall not covet your neighbor's house.
10. You shall not covet your neighbor's wife, servants, animals or anything that belongs to your neighbor.

THE MAIN PURPOSES OF THE LAW (TEN COMMANDMENTS)

It is not the purpose of this Law to save man, because God had already given the promise of salvation through Christ Jesus to Abraham four hundred and thirty years before (see Galatians 3:14-18).

The Law is like a mirror to show us our sins. Since the fall of man into sin by Adam and Eve, the main purpose of the Law is to show us that we are sinners against the will of God. It shows us clearly that we cannot be saved by trying to do self-righteous deeds by our own merit; it helps us to see and recognize ourselves for who we are. The Law makes us realize our lost condition and the need for a Savior (see Romans 7:24). "What a wretched man I am! Who will rescue me from this body of death?" The answer comes in Romans 8:1-2, "Therefore, there is now no condemnation for those who are in Christ Jesus, because through Christ Jesus the law of the Spirit of life set me free from the law of sin and death."

The Law serves as a guide in our lives. To God's children (believers) the Law becomes a guide or a rule, which directs and guides us by pointing out what is genuinely good and pleasing in the sight of God (see Romans 12:1-2). "Therefore, I urge you, brothers, in view of God's mercy, to offer your bodies as living sacrifices, holy and pleasing to God – this is your spiritual act of worship. Do not conform any longer to the pattern of this world, but be transformed by the renewing of your mind. Then you will be able to test and approve what God's will is – his pleasing and perfect will."

The Law serves as a curb to keep order within Society. The Law is mainly intended for the lawless or the disobedient, ungodly, intentional sinners (1 Timothy 1:9-10). For such ungodly the Law with its threat of punishment is to act as a curb, which restrains, holds back and checks such out burst of sin.

SUMMARY

As Christians we rejoice in God's word as recorded by the apostle Paul in Romans 6:14, "For sin shall not be your master, because you are not under the law, but under grace."

This does not allow us to disregard or ignore the Law. We have God's promise that we are saved by His grace and in this grace we live and do God's will out of love because of all His love and blessing to us. We can't earn salvation by keeping His Law. This was done for us by Jesus when He died on the cross for all our sins. Jesus fulfilled the Law for us, so that we could receive the free gift of ETERNAL LIFE. If we were perfect and able to obey the Law, we could be saved. The problem is that we all fall short of perfection and need salvation through Jesus Christ as recorded in Romans 3: 23 and 24. "for all have sinned and fall short of the glory of God, and are justified freely by his grace through the redemption that came by Christ Jesus."

CHAPTER NINE:
PRAYER

Prayer could be summarized as a heart to heart talk with God. A person who has become a child of God (Christian) has a spiritual desire to speak with their Heavenly Father. In our prayers we thank and praise God for all of the blessings which we receive daily and ask Him for special needs. Again, we get direction on prayer from the Scriptures. Philippians 4:6 says, "Do not be anxious about anything, but in everything, by prayer and petition, with thanksgiving, present your requests to God." We are not to worry about our needs or troubles, but we can take them to the Lord in prayer. Our requests must be in agreement with the promises of God, and especially subject to His will. We can't impose our will to God. According to 1 John 5:14 we have God's promise that, if we ask anything according to His will, He hears us. In Luke 11:13, God promises to give us spiritual blessings. "If you then, though you are evil, know how to give good gifts to your children, how much more will your Father in heaven give the Holy Spirit to those who ask him."

We can ask God for things which we need or even things we want if it is in line with God's will for our temporal life, just as we do in the Lord's Prayer, when we say, "Give us this day our daily bread." This includes all the things we need in life such as food, water, clothing, shelter, income, health, good friends, etc. We should not only pray for ourselves but also for others who are in need.

It is God's will that we pray to God the Father and conclude our prayer in the name of Jesus, according to John 16:23. It is important that we pray with a believing heart and firmly believe that our requests are indeed heard by Him, according to James 1:6. "But when he asks, he must believe and not doubt." Christians are always in the spirit of prayer, always grateful for blessings received from God. Christians are fully aware that the Holy Spirit lives within their soul (Ephesians 6:18). It is the Holy Spirit who helps us with our prayers and what we need to pray for, according to Romans 8:26. "In the same way, the Spirit helps us in our weakness. We do not know what we ought to pray for, but the Spirit himself intercedes for us with groans that words cannot express."

What a blessing to know that the Holy Spirit helps us to pray for the things that we and others need.

God answers every proper prayer, but only in His own way and at His own time. For example, when Mary the mother of Jesus told Him that they have no more wine, His reply was "my time has not yet come" (John 2:4).

Also, Paul prayed to God to remove "the thorn in the flesh", but God did not remove it. Instead He gave Paul the strength to endure it saying, "My grace is sufficient for you." (2 Corinthians 12:9)

As we pray to God in faith, and trust in Him to care for us, He calms our fears and assists us in handling our problems and concerns with the full assurance that with God, nothing is impossible. We are not alone. He is there for us to lean on. If God did not spare His only son, but offered Him as a sacrifice to guarantee eternal life, surely He will generously provide for sufficient needs to sustain us on this earth until He takes us to our eternal home with Him in Heaven .This is confirmed in Matt. 6: 25 to 34 where Jesus tells us not to worry about what we will eat or drink or wear.

THE LORD'S PRAYER

When Jesus disciples (followers) asked Lord teach us to pray, Jesus taught them what has become known as the Lord's Prayer as recorded in Matthew 6:9-13 and Luke 11:2-4. This is a most profound yet simple expression of the faith which every Christian has the privilege of praying, completely in line with God's will for us as Jesus taught. The most commonly used words are as follows:

1. Our Father who art in heaven,
2. hallowed be thy name,
3. thy kingdom come,
4. thy will be done on earth as it is in heaven.
5. Give us this day our daily bread;
6. and forgive us our trespasses (sins) as we forgive those who trespass (sin) against us;
7. and lead us not into temptation, but deliver us from evil.

8. For thine is the kingdom and the power and the glory forever and ever. Amen.

In order to help you understand the meaning and depth of this prayer, I have summarized some of Luther's teachings as I understand them.

1. God wants us to believe that He is our true heavenly Father, and that we are His true children, so that we can pray to Him in confidence as a child to their father. This becomes a very personal relationship. He loves us as His children and we love Him as our Father.

2. God's name is holy, but we pray that it may also be holy among us. That we respect His name and not abuse it in our conversations.

3. God's kingdom will definitely come as promised and we pray that it will come especially to us. This happens when we receive the Holy Spirit, so that by His grace we believe His holy word, which leads to eternity with God.

4. Because of the devil and all of the evil in this world, we sometimes make bad choices left on our own. Our prayer is that God's will be done on this earth and we need His will to strengthen our faith and keep us firmly in His word.

5. We ask God to provide for everything we need to support and maintain our body but also to provide other essentials such as family, friends, good weather, honest government, peace, health, ability to earn income, etc.

6. God sets a high standard for us. We don't deserve His forgiveness but He promises to forgive all our sins if we repent and believe in Jesus as our Savior. Our pledge to God is that we in turn will forgive those people who have wronged us. We need God's help to forgive those who wrong us, just as He forgives us for all the wrongs we do.

7. God does not tempt us, but we pray that God would guard and keep us safe so that the devil, the world and our sinful nature would not lead us into doing wrong but receive strength to overcome evil in our lives. 2 Timothy 4:18 says, "The Lord will rescue me from every evil attack and will bring me safely to his heavenly kingdom."

8. We can be certain that this prayer is acceptable to God our Heavenly Father. He has commanded us to pray and He has promised to hear us. We acknowledge God's supernatural power and His mighty works and power. He is eternal and will reign forever. AMEN.

OTHER PRAYERS

Here are a few suggestions to help you with your prayer life.

1.   Evening Prayer

My favorite prayer which I, and my wife Jean of fifty six years, pray each night following the reading of Portals of Prayer (Concordia Publishing House) which aids our devotional life, is Martin Luther's Evening Prayer.

> "I thank You, my heavenly Father, through Jesus Christ, Your dear Son, that You have graciously kept me this day; and I pray You would forgive me all my sins where I have done wrong, and graciously keep me this night. For into Your hands I commend myself, my body and soul, and all things. Let Your holy angel be with me, that the evil foe may have no power over me." Amen. NOTE: You can add any special prayers appropriate regarding health issues or other special needs for you or your family or friends.

2.   Morning Prayer

You can repeat the above prayer and just substitute the word "night" for "day". Again, include any special requests for challenges which you may encounter during the day.

3. Mealtime Prayer

Again, the favorite prayer for my wife and I is the common table prayer which we always repeat together before we eat, even if we are in a restaurant.

> "Come Lord Jesus be thou our guest and let this food to us be blessed."

A more formal prayer could be useful if you have guests over.

> "Gracious Heavenly Father, we thank you for all of your blessings this day. Bless our guests and our fellowship together. Bless our food which we are about to receive through your bountiful goodness. Amen. NOTE: You can add your guest's names and any special occasion such as a birthday or anniversary.

4. Health Concerns

If you are visiting someone who is ill at their home or in hospital it is always appropriate to have a special prayer for them.

"Gracious Heavenly Father, we pray for your special blessings on _____ who is struggling with _____.
We pray that you would touch him (her) with your healing power. Be with the doctors and caregivers as they help with the healing process. We pray for your help and blessings in the name of Jesus our Lord and Savior, Amen."

5. *General Prayers*

As Christians, the blessing is ours to be able to pray to God daily at anytime regarding special needs or special challenges, giving God thanks for the blessings we receive. I.E., When I travel I always try to remember to pray for safety while driving in my car or flying. Again, I try to remember to thank God for keeping me safe when I arrive at my destination.

By making prayer a regular part of our day, we are able to communicate with God as our Father. He wants to hear from you. He cares for you and will provide for your needs according to His will. Listen to God's promises. James 5:16 says, "Therefore, confess your sins to each other and pray for each other so that you may be healed. The prayer of a righteous man is powerful and effective." Also, Psalm 145:18-19 says, "The Lord is near to all who call on him, to all who call on him in truth. He

44

fulfills the desires of those who fear him; he hears their cry and saves them."

The greatest gift and blessing we receive from God is Eternal life as outlined earlier. How pleasing it must be to God when we remember to thank Him daily for this the greatest and most precious gift of all.

CHAPTER TEN:
GOD'S DIRECTION FOR OBTAINING ETERNAL LIFE IN HEAVEN

We have already shown from Scripture that we can not earn or buy our way into Heaven. Eternal life is not achieved by all the good things we do or the bad things we try not to do. Although some believe that Jesus is just one way among many to get to Heaven. Such a belief isn't based on Scripture.

Scripture teaches there is only one way which God Himself provided for all people. Let's start with Acts 4:12 where Peter is talking about Jesus. "Salvation is found in no one else, for there is no other name under heaven given to men by which we must be saved." Jesus suffered death on the cross in place of each one of us and that is the only means of access to God. God provided this plan of access which we can choose to reject. However it is revealed in Scripture for us to receive. As God's word of promise (the Scriptures) brings faith to our hearts, we receive Him on His terms.

The process begins when we recognize that we are all sinful and it is our sin that prohibits us from obtaining eternal life with God. We are born with a nature that is full of sin and because of this sinful nature our entire being responds with thoughts, words and actions that are sinful. This we learn from the scriptures. Romans 3:23 tells us, "For all have sinned and fall short of the Glory of God."

Romans 3:10-11 tells us that no one is righteous. As it is written, "There is no one righteous, not even one; there is no one who understands, no one who seeks God." We need to confess that we are sinful. We need to acknowledge that because of our sinful nature we are not deserving of being in God's perfect presence in death, but God in love provides us with the free gift of eternal life. Here is the good news from Scripture. Romans 6:23 says, "For the wages of sin is death, but the gift of God is eternal life in Christ Jesus our Lord."

We need to believe God's plan of salvation for us in that Christ died on the cross for us. Ephesians 1:7 tells us, "In him (Jesus) we have redemption through his blood, the forgiveness of sins, in accordance with the riches of God's grace."

It is evident that Christ paid an awesome price for our salvation. His sacrifice of dying for our sins is a free gift for us, but cost Him everything. John 3:36 gives us that assurance to believe that eternal life is ours, which sates this as something we must believe. "Whoever believes in the Son has eternal life, but whoever rejects the Son will not see life, for God's wrath remains on him."

Jesus himself gives us His personal assurance in John 10:28, where He refers to believers as His sheep. "I give them eternal life, and they shall never perish; no one can snatch them out of my hand."

SUMMARY

God's will and desire for us is to admit that we are in fact sinful and that our sins separate us from Him. But He is a God of love and, when we repent of all our sins, He forgives us all of our sins. He forgives us because Jesus suffered death on the cross on our behalf and so God gives us eternal life because we have faith and trust in His promises to us.

When you and I believe that Jesus died and rose for us, we can with full assurance and confidence trust in Jesus Christ for our eternal life.

Again, the scriptures are very clear about faith in Jesus. Here are three scripture passages which give this assurance to us.

Romans 10:17 – "Consequently, faith comes from hearing the message, and the message is heard through the word of Christ."

Acts 16:31 – "Believe in the Lord Jesus, and you will be saved – you and your household."

John 20:31 – But these (miracles) are written that you may believe that Jesus is the Christ, the Son of God, and that by believing you may have life in his name."

What a blessing to believe and know that we can look forward to eternal life in Heaven with God when we die. As you learn and receive Jesus as your Savior, you can be confident that God has in fact brought you to faith, and you become a child of God. As His child you can spend the rest of your earthly life living in peace and joy thanking God and serving Him daily to the best of your ability. This service is done in love and in response to God's free gift of eternal life to you.

CHAPTER ELEVEN:
CONFESSION AND ABSOLUTION OF YOUR SINS

As part of an ongoing faith life that trusts in God, it is important and necessary that we regularly acknowledge and confess all of our sins to God, even those which we do not know. You can do this as part of a regular worship service or you can do this privately. Again, we go to the Scriptures for direction. 1 John 1:8-9 says, "If we claim to be without sin, we deceive ourselves and the truth is not in us. If we confess our sins, he is faithful and just and will forgive us our sins and purify us from all unrighteousness."

Some churches provide opportunity to confess your sins in private to their Priest or Pastor. This is a helpful means to confess those sins which you are aware of and feel in your heart. You then receive the comforting assurance that your sins are forgiven, according to God's promises. Some Christian churches have a general confession and absolution as part of their regular Sunday worship.

The following is a sample prayer of Confession and Absolution which you can use for your own personal use.

> Gracious Heavenly Father, I confess that I am sinful and that I daily fail to live up to the standards which you have given to us

in the Ten Commandments and in your Scriptures. I have not loved you with my whole heart and I have not loved those in my life according to your will. I realize that my sins separate me from you and I desire your forgiveness. I ask that you remove all the sin in my life and cleanse me as you have promised to me and to all sinners who are repentant. Cover me with the robe of righteousness that Jesus won for me with His life, suffering and dying on the cross and His resurrection from the dead. I accept Jesus as my Lord and Savior. This I ask in the name of Jesus. Amen.

ABSOLUTION OR THE FORGIVENESS OF YOUR SINS

Hear the good news from the word of the Lord as recorded in Isaiah 1:18. "Though your sins are like scarlet, they shall be as white as snow; though they be red as crimson, they shall be like wool."

In public Worship, the words of absolution may be similar to the following.

Jesus has paid the price for all of your sins and makes you whole. God has indeed heard your confession and knows the sincerity of your heart. As a redeemed child of God, it is my privilege to pronounce God's grace to you. Because of His life, death and resurrection, and by His authority to forgive sin, I assure you the full forgiveness of all of your sins in the name of the Father and the Son and the Holy Spirit. You now are also a child of God, redeemed by your faith. Go and live in joy, knowing that you have received God's grace and the free gift of eternal life. Serve others and share your faith knowing that God is with you.

The angels in Heaven rejoice for every sinner who repents according to Luke 15:10. Your name is entered into the book of life which guarantees God's promise of ETERNAL LIFE in HEAVEN.

CHAPTER TWELVE:

FREE PASSPORT TO HEAVEN

God loves you and wants you to enjoy the assurance and blessings of Eternal Life in Heaven. You can receive this free gift by understanding and accepting God's plan of salvation which includes the following truths which have already been explained in this book.

1. Eternal Life cannot be earned or obtained by any good deed or personal merit. Eternal Life in Heaven is an absolute free gift, given by God because of His love and amazing Grace. Grace is something you receive when you don't deserve it. This is confirmed in Ephesians 2:8, "For it is by grace you have been saved, through faith and not from yourselves, it is the gift of God."

2. Everyone is a sinner, which includes me and you. You and I were born with original sin and because of this sinful nature we do sinful acts which are contrary to God's Ten Commands and God's will. Your sin and mine prohibits us (and all people) from obtaining Eternal Life with God. This is confirmed in Romans 3:10-12. "There is no one righteous, not even one; there is no one who understands, no one who seeks God. All have turned away, they have become worthless; there is no one who does good, not even one."

3. Scripture helps us to understand God and teaches us that He is a just God and therefore He does not overlook our sin. He must deal with it. He is patient and loving toward us and does not want to punish us as we deserve. The Holy Bible reveals God to us. Romans 2:11 says, "For God does not show favoritism." But promises a summary of His involvement with the world in my favorite Bible passage, the Gospel in a nutshell in John 3:16-17, "For God so loved the world that he gave his one and only Son, that whoever believes in him shall not perish but have eternal life. For God did not send his Son into the world to condemn the world, but to save the world through him."

4. In all of this it is important to understand who Jesus is. He is true God who became true man in order that for once a man might live the perfect life. This is difficult for us to understand but Scriptures teach that Jesus was both God and man in one person. He was sinless, but because of His love for us, He took all our sins upon Himself. As God in human flesh, He willingly died on the cross full of our sin deserving death. But because He was God in human flesh, in dying for our sins, Jesus did not remain in the grip of death. This is the good news of the Gospel. Jesus, being also God, rose from the dead on the third day and proved that God has total power over death. Again, the scriptures confirm all of this.

5. In John 1:1,14, we read, "In the beginning was the Word, and the Word was with God, and the Word was God. The Word because flesh and made his dwelling among us. We have seen his glory, the glory of the One and Only who came from the Father, full of grace and truth." Also, in John 14:6, Jesus is speaking to His disciples, "I am the way the truth and the life. No one comes to the Father except through me."

6. Finally, you need to know and understand how you can obtain God's free gift of ETERNAL LIFE. As previously mentioned, God wants you to personally admit that you are sinful and acknowledge that your sins separate you from Him. Next when you ask God to forgive all of your sins, He in fact does so because Jesus paid the penalty for all of your sins. He died on the cross for your sins and then was raised to life on the third day to proclaim final victory over death so that you and all believers can obtain ETERNAL LIFE.

You can claim your FREE GIFT of ETERNAL LIFE and victory over death by FAITH. When you believe that Jesus died and rose again for you, then you are a CHRISTIAN who places your total confidence and trust in JESUS CHRIST for your ETERNAL LIFE.

Again, we go to the HOLY BIBLE to confirm what the scriptures say about faith in JESUS. 1 John 5:11-13 says, "And this is the testimony: God has given us eternal life, and this life is in the Son. He who has the Son has life; he who does not have the Son of God does not have life. I write these things to you who believe in the name of the Son of God so that you may know that you have eternal life."

Romans 10:17 – Paul is speaking to the Romans. "Consequently, faith comes from hearing the message, and the message is heard through the word of Christ."

(Acts 16:31) Paul is responding to the jailer who asked, "What must I do to be saved," in verse 30. The reply by Paul in verse 31 is, "Believe in the Lord Jesus, and you will be saved." Later Paul and Silas spoke the word of God to the Jailer and he and his family were baptized. This confirms the power of God's word in bringing you and all repentant sinners to Faith.

The Holy Spirit works in your heart through God's word and brings you to faith. God's word helps you to acknowledge your sins and to confess your sins to God and believe that He forgives all of your sins. You are no longer a sinner separated from God, but now you are a FORGIVEN SINNER, and have become a CHILD OF GOD. You have become a new Christian and as

Your life now has real purpose as you reflect God's love for you in your service to Him and to others in your life. This assurance of eternal life is our only source of true peace.

You can now be at peace and know for sure that you will indeed go to Heaven when your last day comes. If you believe in this gift of God through Jesus, rejoice, you are now a believer in Christ, your sins are forgiven, the Holy Spirit lives in your soul. You are born again spiritually. We can confirm all of this in John 1:12. "Yet to all who received him, to those who believed in his name, he gave the right to become children of God." This verse confirms your membership in God's family by God's grace because of your faith in God.

Because of your faith and trust in God, and because of your confession of all your sins, and because of your belief that Jesus suffered and died for all your sins and that He is your Lord and Savior, and because you want to change your life as a child of God, you have God's assurance of ETERNAL LIFE in HEAVEN. You may now want to personalize your faith and trust in God by signing the PASSPORT TO HEAVEN on the next page.

A word of explanation regarding this PASSPORT to HEAVEN. This is not a biblical requirement. It is intended to serve as a personal declaration of your FAITH in GOD who gives and provides free access to HEAVEN through JESUS. By completing it, you formally demonstrate your acceptance of God's Grace for your life.

It may be helpful for you to regularly read this PASSPORT to remind you of your commitment and of God's blessings to you in this life and your Eternal Life in HEAVEN.

You have become a new Christian and as His Spirit works faith in your heart, you desire to live a Christian life.

VISAS

PASSPORT TO HEAVEN

Freely awarded to

_____   _____
Print your name   Date

BASED ON YOUR PERSONAL
CONFESSION AND COMMITMENT
TO CHRISTIANITY

Because God, through Jesus Christ has forgiven me (2 Cor. 5:18-20), and because through the power of the Holy Spirit I am a new creation called to love (2 Cor. 5:17), and by God's power in me and by His grace I commit myself to God, to guide and direct me according to His will. (2 Cor. 5:15) "and he died for all, that those who live should no longer live for themselves but for him who died for them and was raised again."

This personal prayer expresses the desire of my heart. Gracious Heavenly Father. Thank you for the gift of eternal life. Because you have sent your Holy Spirit into my heart I believe that Jesus is the Son of God and that He died for all my sins and rose again from the dead. I now put my complete trust in you alone for eternal life according to your promises. With your help I want to do your will. May other people come to know You as their Lord through me. Thank you for saving me. In Jesus' name. AMEN.

Signature

_____Rev.2:10B
"Be faithful, even to the point of death, and I will give you the crown of life."

CHAPTER THIRTEEN:

WHAT IS THE CHRISTIAN PURPOSE FOR LIFE ON THIS EARTH?

Finally after claiming Jesus as our Savior from sin and death, our purpose in life is affected. The average person tends to struggle with what their purpose in life is all about. Is it the "American dream", which puts a lot of emphasis on materialism? A lot of time and energy is put into keeping up with the Joneses. For many, it's all about us and what we have and want, hoping that the more we have the happier we will be. Unfortunately, this usually has the opposite effect and does not provide the joy and peace of mind we are looking for. We need to seek God's direction regarding what He desires for us.

In Luke 12:22-30, Jesus tells His disciples and all of us not to worry about our lives regarding what we will eat or what we will wear. In verse 31, He says "<u>But seek his kingdom,</u> and these things will be given to you as well." <u>We need to connect with Jesus to give our life purpose.</u> Jesus is the vine and we are the branches, according to John 15:5. God is the gardener and he prunes us (the branches) so that we will be even more fruitful. We are to bear much fruit which gives God glory according to John 15:8. Once we have connected with Jesus (receiving Him as our Lord and Savior) we become part of God's family. This is confirmed in 1 John 3:1. "How great is the love the Father has lavished on us, that we should be called children of God! And that is what we are!"

As children of God we receive many blessings from our Heavenly Father. Besides providing us with all our needs on this earth (Phil. 4:19), we also receive a special inheritance which is eternal life with God in Heaven. John 6:40 says, "For my Father's will is that everyone who looks to the Son and believes in him shall have eternal life, and I will raise him up at the last day."

<u>All of these blessings give us a special purpose in our life to serve Christ and to reflect Him in our lives.</u> Again, God gives us direction for the kind of service he requires from His followers:

- Ephesians 2:10, "For we are God's workmanship, created in Christ to do good works, which God prepared in advance for us to do.

- In Matthew 26 verse 34-40, Jesus wants His followers to care for the needy, those who are hungry and thirsty or in need of clothes. Help strangers, visit and care for the sick, visit those in prison. In verse 40, Jesus says, "The King will reply, 'I tell you the truth, whatever you did for one of the least of these brothers of mine, you did for me."

- Luke 6:31 – Jesus is speaking. "Do to others as you would have them do to you."

- Luke 10:30-37 – Jesus gives us the parable of the Good Samaritan which teaches us to show kindness to others. As Christians we are to love God with all our heart, soul, strength and mind and to love our neighbors as ourselves according to Luke 10:27. We are to be a living testimony of what God has done for us. We do this by showing kindness to others in need with love and compassion.

Our deeds of love reflect our faith and trust in God. Jesus suffered and died on the cross for all of our sins. This is how He showed His love for us. We reflect our love for Him through the good deeds we do to others on His behalf. This we do with a joyful heart knowing that we have received the free gift of Eternal Life through FAITH in JESUS. The apostle Paul sums up our service to God very clearly in Galatians 6:18, and then we are encouraged in verse 9 and 10 as follows: "Let us not become weary in doing good, for at the proper time we will reap a harvest if we do not give up." Therefore, as we have opportunity, let us do good to all people, especially to those who belong to the family of believers.

Faith without works is a dead faith, but true faith in God is alive. It is more than a feeling, it is also doing. When we see a need, it's an opportunity to respond in Christian love. Even small things can make a difference to a person in need.

<u>This leads us into the next purpose for us and that is</u> <u>to SHARE THE GOSPEL,</u> telling others the good news of salvation through Jesus. We love to share all kinds of news, why not share the life changing news about your faith in God! That Heaven is a free gift from God if we believe and trust in Jesus as our Savior. Let's go to the scriptures and get encouragement and direction from God.

1 Peter 2:9 – "But you are a chosen people, a royal priesthood, a holy nation, a people belonging to God, that you may declare the praises of him who called you out of darkness into his wonderful light."

1 Peter 3:15-16 – "But in your hearts set apart Christ as Lord. Always be prepared to give an answer to everyone who asks you to give the reason for the hope that you have. But do this with gentleness and respect."

Then in Matthew 28:18-20, we have the Great Commission from Jesus as He talks to His disciples following His resurrection from the dead. Then Jesus came to them and said, "All authority in heaven and on earth has been given to me. Therefore go and make disciples of all nations, baptizing them in the name of the Father and of the Son and of the Holy Spirit, and teaching them to obey everything I have commanded you. And surely I am with you always, to the very end of the age."

Once we are connected to God, we have a whole new purpose to connect others to God. This is not an easy task but it can be done especially in our circle of influence of trusted relationships with family, relatives and friends. In my case, I have decided that I will reach out to others through this small book in hopes that this message will connect them to Jesus in a positive way.

Summary of Life's Purpose

There are many purposes for our life. I agree that it is important to get the best education possible, to get a job that is satisfying and pays well so you can provide for yourself and your family. God wants us to be good stewards of our resources; However, my goal is to get your thoughts beyond the temporal things of this earth, and that is to provide not only for this world but also for eternity. The best is yet to come and that's ETERNAL LIFE IN HEAVEN and we need to prepare for that. In Luke 16:26, Jesus says, "What good will it be for a man if he gains the whole world, yet forfeits his soul?"

I mentioned three important purposes for our life:

1. Connecting to Jesus
2. Serving God with good deeds to others
3. Sharing the good news of the Gospel

Here are some suggestions for connecting to Jesus:

1. Join a Christian church that teaches according to the truth of the Scriptures. I have been an active member of First Lutheran Church, Kelowna, BC, for 44

years. This is where I connect with Jesus and grow in my faith through God's word, Confessing and receiving Absolution of sins, experiencing the sacrament of Holy Communion, singing praises to God, studying Scripture and joining with others in Christian fellowship. Our Mission Statement is to be a Congregation that is "Sharing the love of Christ with all people, empowering them to live life, in faith, to the fullest now and forever." We have grown from a staff of one (the pastor) to a church staff of eight, a Preschool staff of five, and a Christian Elementary School staff of fifteen. You can check out what we believe on our website at www.firstlutheran.ca. We have a traditional service with liturgy, organ music and singing of hymns, plus we have a contemporary service with a Praise Team, which attracts younger families and children. The same Christian message is used but it is presented differently to meet the needs of all generations

If you are interested in checking out a Lutheran Church in your area call Lutheran Hour Ministries at 1-800-876-9880. This is an auxiliary organization of The Lutheran Church Missouri_ Synod in the U.S. and Lutheran Church_ Canada, of which I am a member. Its primary purpose is to proclaim the Gospel around the world mainly over radio during the past 80 years. The weekly broadcast covers approximately 120 countries in nearly 40 languages. The organization is dedicated in "Bringing Christ to the Nations and the Nations to the Church." If you are interested in downloading or printing copies of weekly sermons or signing up for daily inspirational devotions, go to this Web site: www.lutheranhour.org.

There are of course many other denominations that are Christian churches. It is important to check out what they believe and teach. Join a bible study group and enroll in a Christianity course where you can learn the basis of the Scriptures and grow in understanding of the Christian faith.

2. Start reading the Bible regularly. Start with the New Testament. I really get a lot of comfort and strength from Romans 8:28-39. In the Old Testament, Genesis and Exodus are a must read, as well as the book of Psalm and Isaiah.

3. For a complete understanding of the main teachings of the Bible, I recommend reading Luther's small Catechism. It is available at Christian Book Stores or in local Libraries. It is also available on the internet.

4. Connect with a small group or find a Christian friend who can help you in your spiritual growth.

CHAPTER FOURTEEN:
THE APOSTLES' CREED

A creed is a brief summary statement of what Christians believe and teach. The earliest written is called the Apostles' Creed because it is a brief statement of the teachings and doctrines of the Apostles as found in the Bible. Many Christian churches have this as a part of their worship service.

> I believe in God the Father Almighty,
> maker of heaven and earth
> And in Jesus Christ, his only Son, our Lord
> who was conceived by the Holy Spirit,
> born of the virgin Mary,
> suffered under Pontius Pilate,
> was crucified, died and was buried.
> He descended into Hell.
> The third day he rose again from the dead.
> He ascended into Heaven
> and sits at the right hand of God
> the Father almighty.
> From thence he will come to judge the living and the dead.
> I believe in the Holy Spirit,
> the holy Christian church,
> the communion of saints,
> the resurrection of the body,
> and the life everlasting. Amen.

The second general Creed of Christendom is the Nicene Creed and the third, and much longer Creed, is the Athanasian Creed. These two Creeds expand considerably the relationship and specific assignments of the three distinct persons of Father, Son and Holy Spirit, which in total form or comprise one Triune God.

Creation of this world as we know is ascribed to the Father.

Jesus the Son, who was begotten of the Father, is ascribed the work of redemption. He became flesh so that he could take our sins upon Himself.

The Holy Spirit, who proceeded from the Father and the Son, is given the power of sanctification, (which is the forgiveness of sins), bringing us to Faith, acting in response to being forgiven and taking our Souls to Heaven when we reach life's end on this earth.

These distinctions are set out clearly in these Creeds so that Christians have a simple and full assurance of the existence of only one Holy Triune God and yet understand the existence of three persons in the Divine Essence of God. These truths have been assembled from the various inspired writings of Moses and the prophets of the Old Testament and from the Apostles in the New Testament.

Naturally there are many critiques regarding these Christian Creeds, however, for almost 2000 years,

Christians have through faith maintained these teachings to be accurate and true.

The Bible clearly defines that God is comprised of three distinct persons, Father, Son and Holy Spirit. In Genesis 1:1-3 we learn of God and of the Spirit of God, and in John 1:1-3 of the Word, by whom all things were made. Because there are more persons than one in the very beginning, God said, "Let us make man in our image, after our likeness." (Genesis 1:26).

We also have proof of the Trinity in the New Testament in Matthew 3:16-17, at the baptism of Christ. As soon as Jesus was baptized, he went up out of the water. At that moment heaven was opened, and he saw the Spirit of God descending like a dove and lighting on him. And a voice from heaven said, "This is my Son, whom I love; with Him I am well pleased."

Also in Matthew 28:19, Jesus is speaking to His disciples. "Therefore go and make disciples of all nations, baptizing them in the name of the Father and of the Son and of the Holy Spirit."

CHAPTER FIFTEEN:
SUMMARY

My intention in this book has been to share God's word from the Bible regarding God's plan of salvation for all people. Salvation is our greatest need because of our sinful nature. The only rescue from sin is found in Jesus according to Acts 4:12, "Salvation is found in no one else, for there is no other name under heaven given to man by which we must be saved."

There is no doubt as to whether the believer in Jesus is saved. We have this guarantee because Jesus earned our salvation for us on the cross. Only Jesus has met and satisfied God's demands of perfection. He lived the perfect life for us, and as the holy and righteous Son of god, He willingly atoned for all our sins through His suffering and death on the cross. By His sacrifice, Jesus made us at one with the Father, reconciling us to Him by His blood and confirmed in 1 John 2:2. "He is the atoning sacrifice for our sins, and not only ours but also for the sins of the whole world."

Heaven is a perfect place where there is no sin. We are not perfect and therefore by ourselves we are not worthy of heaven. The good news is that we are made perfect in God's eyes through Jesus. He qualified us by taking all of our sins upon Himself to the cross! Just before He died, His last words were, "It is finished." His death paid for all of our sins.

But Jesus didn't stay dead in the grave, He rose from the dead on the third day to prove power over death and guarantee us Eternal Life when we die physically. Death is not the end for the Christian; it is a stepping stone to Heaven. For us the best is yet to come. It is important that all people believe in Jesus Christ, God's only Son, as God's only way to receive Eternal Life. To trust in yourself or anyone else is to miss God's only provision for reconciliation with Him. Why gamble with your eternal life. Allow the Holy Spirit to work faith in your heart. What a joy to those who put their trust in God and accept Jesus as their personal Savior. What a joy to receive forgiveness for all your sins. What a joy to have certainty of eternal life.

May you enjoy God's love and peace in your life.

Receive the Blessing of the Lord as you continue to study His word and His love for you. "The Lord bless you and keep you. The Lord make his face shine on you and be gracious to you. The Lord look upon you with favor and give you peace. Amen."

In conclusion, this is my hope for you. May the Holy Spirit dwell within you to strengthen your faith and trust in God, and may you live in confidence knowing that you are never alone as you enjoy a purpose filled life, serving your Savior.

Thanks be to God for the blessings of this life and especially for the free gift of ETERNAL LIFE in HEAVEN. AMEN.

CHAPTER SIXTEEN:
ABOUT THE AUTHOR

HAROLD W. DECKSHEIMER, KELOWNA, BC, CANADA

Harold Decksheimer was born in Cupar, Saskatchewan in 1933. After high school in Dysart, Sask, he went to work in Moose Jaw, Sask, in 1951 for Crown Lumber Company as a trainee for future management. This worked out well and the company transferred Harold to Calgary in 1960, Vancouver area in 1965 and to Kelowna, BC, in 1966, as an Administrator/Controller for the Interior of B.C. Harold received his degree as a Certified Management Accountant (CMA) in 1971.

After twenty one years with this company, Harold went into the Retail Shoe business with his wife Jean, in 1972. He needed a different challenge so turned the management of the business over to his wife and went to work for Western Star Trucks. He worked there for seventeen years in several management positions which included Controller, Production Manager, Personnel Director and Senior Financial Analyst. He retired in 1990 but continued to work there as a part-time consultant for five more years.

Christianity in my Life

This is my story. I was baptized in the Lutheran Church in North Cupar, Sask, as an infant. Later, at age fifteen, I attended confirmation classes where I was taught the basics of Christianity by our Pastor, using Luther's Small Catechism. I studied all of the key teachings of the Bible which included the Ten Commandments, The Apostles' Creed, the Lord's Prayer, the Sacrament of Holy Baptism, Confession and Absolution of Sins, the Sacrament of the Altar (Holy Communion) and memorized over one hundred key Bible verses. I had a very strong faith in God and received Jesus as my personal Savior. This training at a young age has stayed with me all of my life and I have enjoyed being very active in my church over the past sixty years. I have been a member of First Lutheran Church in Kelowna for forty four years. I was blessed to be in active leadership in serving in the roles of Director of Stewardship, Director of Lay Ministry (assisting the Pastor) and served as Executive Director (President) of the Congregation off and on for twenty five years.

I am thankful for the opportunity to teach hundreds of Bible classes at the church and in my home. I've had the privilege of serving as a Lay Pastor, leading the Sunday worship services when the Pastor was away or on vacation. I've probably conducted about fifty services over the past forty years using sermons from Lutheran Hour speakers or from a Book of Sermons and amending them to fit our local message needs. Each Sermon always contained enough law to show us that we are sinners in need of a Savior, and provided the Good News of the Gospel, that Jesus suffered and died on the cross for all of our sins and rose from the dead to conquer death so that we could be assured of Eternal Life.

One of my greatest joys as a Christian has been to serve God and our church through Lutheran Hour Ministries, which is an auxiliary organization of the Lutheran Church Missouri Synod in the U.S. and Lutheran Church Canada, in Canada.

The World Headquarters is located in St. Louis, Missouri and operate in more than 30 countries. These Ministry centers use radio and television programming, print and internet materials, Bible Courses, drama, music, mass evangelism and other culturally appropriate methods to share Christ's message of hope with those who need to hear it. I have served on the International Board of Directors, the Canadian Board of Directors, Regional District President, Zone President, Club President and currently serve as the local Congregational Ambassador. This Ministry has really helped me to understand Christianity and its World Wide scope, to know that Christians are spread all over this world. The current number of Christians is estimated to be 2.1 billion which represents approximately 31 % of the current world population.

Another blessing in my life happened about ten years ago in 2000 when I was approached by two of the directors of the Kelowna Gospel Mission to assist them in a Management/Consultant roll for an interim period, as they were in need of a permanent Manager for the Kelowna Gospel Mission Hostel. I served in this interim capacity for three months. My assignment was to create unity among the staff of sixteen and to assist the Directors in recruiting a full time Manager/Director, who would report to the Board of Directors. At that time the Gospel Mission provided about 100 meals per day to street people, provided shelter to approximately 40 men each night, had a shelter for women in a separate location and a Thrift Store to provide clothes and basic needs to the poor. With much prayer and God's help I was successful in the task assigned to me. A young Pastor was one of several applicants who we hired and I am pleased to see that he is still there and the Gospel Mission is growing under his Christian leadership. I learned to appreciate the words of Jesus, that as we feed and care for the poor and needy we are in fact doing it unto Him.

I have been blessed to be a Christian all of my life. I have been fed spiritually by attending church services regularly. I have the joy and peace in my life which comes from God's love through His word and sacraments. I will continue to share God's love with others until the Lord calls me home into His Heavenly mansions.

My prayer is that God will do the same for you.

Author, Harold W. Decksheimer

CPSIA information can be obtained at www.ICGtesting.com
Printed in the USA
LVOW132241240412

278971LV00001B/4/P